Creative Writing Workbook

By Lynn Grahame

Published by English with

Copyright © English with Lynn 2023

Cartoon characters designed by Gnei Abirami Inasha
Cover designed by GetCovers

Images by Siggy Nowak © Pixabay on pages 7,10, 61
Images by Joe © Pixabay on pages 14, 30, 58
Image by Kinkate © Pixabay on page 20
Images by 小满 郭 © Pixabay on pages 25,
Image by Petra © Pixabay on pages 27,
Image by Эльвина Якубова © Pixabay on page 37
Images by Noel Bauza © Pixabay on pages 56, 89
Image by Arek Socha © Pixabay on pages 60
Images by Enrique Meseguer © Pixabay on pages 68, 71, 93
Images by Peter Fischer © Pixabay on pages 77, 81, 85
Image by S Ford © on page 24

www.englishwithlynn.co.uk

No part of this publication may be reproduced, stored, or transmitted in any form or by any means without the prior written permission of the author, except for permitted uses in accordance with UK copyright law.

My name is Lynn. I have a passion for teaching children. I find it very rewarding to see children grow in confidence whilst teaching them the skills they need to flourish and succeed.

I have been a primary school teacher since 1999. I have worked in a number of primary schools, in a variety of settings, with a wide range of abilities.

In 2017, I left the classroom to travel around South East Asia. It is here that I started to teach online. When I returned to the United Kingdom, I decided to continue teaching this way and realised I enjoyed tutoring creative writing and grammar skills the most.

When teaching creative writing, I noticed that whilst some children have a certain flair in their use of language; many struggle with the use of literary devices and fall back onto a bank of pre-learned phrases and words. This book encourages children to think about their vocabulary and sentence structures. It shows the students a method of planning that incorporates plot and language, enabling a smoother transition into story writing.

After the success of my 'Spelling, Punctuation and Grammar workbook', I decided to write a creative writing book. The aim of this is to help children in lower key stage 2 to develop the skills they gained from my 'SPAG book.

I hope this book will give the children the confidence and independence they need to write fluent, creative stories.

Notes for parents - How to use this book   05
Join the team - Notes for children   06
How to annotate images - notes before you begin   07

Literary devices to use in your writing

How to create expanded noun phrases   08
How to create similes   11
How to use onomatopoeia   15
Creating alliteration effectively   18
Introducing personification   21
Using body language to show feelings   25
Using the senses   28

Sentences

What are clauses and phrases?   31
The three types of sentence structures   35
Using a where sentence starter   38
Using a when sentence starter   41
Using an emotion word starter   44
Using an ing sentence starter   47
Using an adverb of manner starter   50

How to…

How to structure your writing into paragraphs   53
How to introduce your setting   56
How to introduce a character   59
How to plan your writing   62
How to write your opening   66
How to write your problem   69
How to write your solution   72

Over to you

How to use this section   76
Story 1 - The race   77
Story 2 - Journey into space   81
Story 3 - The wizard   85
Story 4 - The camping trip   89
Other story titles you can use   93

Helpful vocabulary sheets

Colour alternatives	94
Adjective synonyms	95
Body language	96
Words linked to the senses	97
Verb synonyms	98
Emotion words	99
Adverbs of manner	100
Synonyms for said	101
Photocopiable planning grid	102
Photocopiable checklist	103

Answers   105

Thank you to the parents and children who have worked through and given feedback on the various sections of this book.

Notes for parents

This creative writing book has been developed for children in lower key stage 2. It explains the literary devices used within story writing, and develops the knowledge that children will have, hopefully, been taught in school. It includes sections on: using literary devices; using different sentence structures; how to plan; and has opportunities for children to write their own stories.

Each topic in this book has 3 sections:

- **Talk Together!**
- **Have a go!**
- **Wrap it up!**

For your child to get the most out of this book, there needs to be interaction between adult and child. The '**Talk Together!**' sections are where you and your child will sit and discuss the topic. At this point, it is important that you encourage your child to ask questions about anything they do not understand.

In the '**Have a go!**' section, encourage your child to be independent in their learning. Once they have finished this section, sit with them and look at the answers. Identify any areas that have misconceptions and look back at the '**Talk together!**' section for clarification.

I would encourage you to sit with your child when they are completing the '**Wrap it up!**' section. By doing this, they can verbally explain their thoughts to you. Once they have explained them, encourage your child to put their ideas into writing.

This book has been written in 4 sections - literary devices, sentence structures, how to... and over to you. I would suggest that your child works through the book in order as the skills learned in the first two sections are needed in the final two sections.

It will be more effective for your child to work through this book one section at a time rather than trying to complete it all at once. This will help them develop a secure understanding of the topic. Once they have completed the whole book, I would suggest that your child revisits each topic to confirm that their knowledge has been retained.

Join the team

Here are the characters that you will meet as you work through this book. Use the final box to include yourself.

Hi! I'm Tom. In my section of this book, you sit with an adult and **'Talk together!'** You need to read the sections and discuss the ideas. This will help you with the other tasks you will do.

Hi! I'm Hameed. In my section you will **'Have a go!'** Once you have talked about the topic, it is time for you to try and answer some questions on your own.

Hi! I'm Rachel. In my section, you will 'Wrap it up!' You will review your understanding by using the skills you have learned in the 'Talk together!' and 'Have a go!' sections.

Hi! I'm Helen. I appear throughout the book. My job is to give you a **'Helpful hint'** about the topics. You will be able to use my hints to help you complete your work.

Hi! I'm _____. I am going to work hard developing my skills. I will discuss the sections with an adult and explain my answers. This will help me improve my understanding.

How to annotate images

The tasks in this book often include images for children to write about. It is helpful if you teach your child how to annotate these images; this will help them to collect different literary devices. This page explains the process of annotating and can be used in many of the tasks throughout this book.

First, look at the image and discuss what nouns can be seen. Include elements of the weather that can't be seen (abstract nouns). Then, write the nouns on the image.

Once the image has been annotated, think about which literary device would be of most use (these are explained in the next section) - you might have several ideas at this stage. Make a list of the ideas below the image.

Your child now has a bank of literary devices ready to include in their writing.

Example

Rocks poking out of the sea like sharp needles (simile)	The wind roared angrily (personification)
Crash! The waves (onomatopoeia)	The sand glistened (description)
The cliffs were as still as a soldier on guard (Simile/personification)	Rough, rugged rocks (alliteration/description)

How to create expanded noun phrases

Talk together!

What is a phrase?

A phrase is a group of words that work together, but do not contain a verb. There are several different types of phrases. In this section we are focusing on expanded noun phrases.

To be able to understand expanded noun phrases, first you need to know what a noun phrase is.

A noun phrase is when you use a **determiner** and a **noun**: '**the boy**'.

By using an **expanded noun phrase** rather than just a **noun phrase** you are giving your reader a clearer image of what the noun is like.

How do we create expanded noun phrases?

An expanded noun phrase is when you use a **determiner** followed by either one or two **adjectives**, separated by a comma, and then the **noun** that the adjectives are describing.

The	ancient, derelict	building
Determiner	adjectives	noun

You can also use a second noun in an expanded noun phrase to give more detail. '**The tree**' is a noun phrase. '**The oak tree**' is an expanded noun phrase. This can be developed further by adding an adjective before the noun.

The	oak	tree
Determiner	noun	noun

The	ancient	oak	tree
Determiner	adjective	noun	noun

8

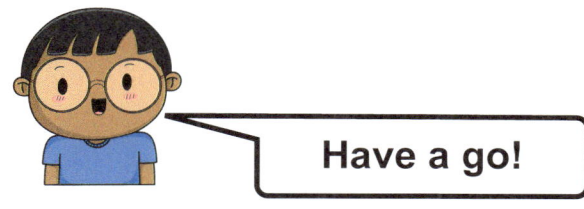

Have a go!

Look at the sentences below. Underline the expanded noun phrases. Try to identify the determiner, the adjectives and the noun. The first one has been done for you.

1. The girl had <u>some sparkly, pink shoes</u> that she wore to the disco.
2. The stripey, blue fish swim quickly through the ocean.
3. The man drove his rusty, old van slowly down the road.
4. My grandmother lives in a pretty, little cottage.
5. The boy brought a new, fluffy jacket.
6. The one-eyed, green alien landed his silver spaceship.
7. The bright green, wooden door slowly creaked open.
8. On Tuesday, the young, mischievous boy went to the park.
9. For dinner, I had some delicious, creamy soup.

Now you are able to identify the expanded noun phrases in sentences. Try to write expanded noun phrases for the following nouns. Experiment with the different types of determiners so you are not always using a, an or the (articles).

Remember to experiment with different adjectives. Try to include synonyms for common words such as big or small.

Determiner	Adjective	,	Adjective	Noun
				castle
				forest
				dragon
				clouds
				goblin

Wrap it up!

Use what you have learned about expanded noun phrases to write phrases about this image. You might find it helpful to annotate the image first.

Helen's helpful hint
You are writing phrases at the minute, not complete sentences. You do not need to include a full stop at the end of a phrase.

How to create similes

Talk together!

A simile is used to make a comparison between two different things using the words '**as**' or '**like**'. Writers use similes to help the reader get a clearer picture in their mind.

It is useful to collect ideas before you begin writing your similes.
If you were going to write a simile about something being hot, it is helpful to collect ideas of things that are hot.

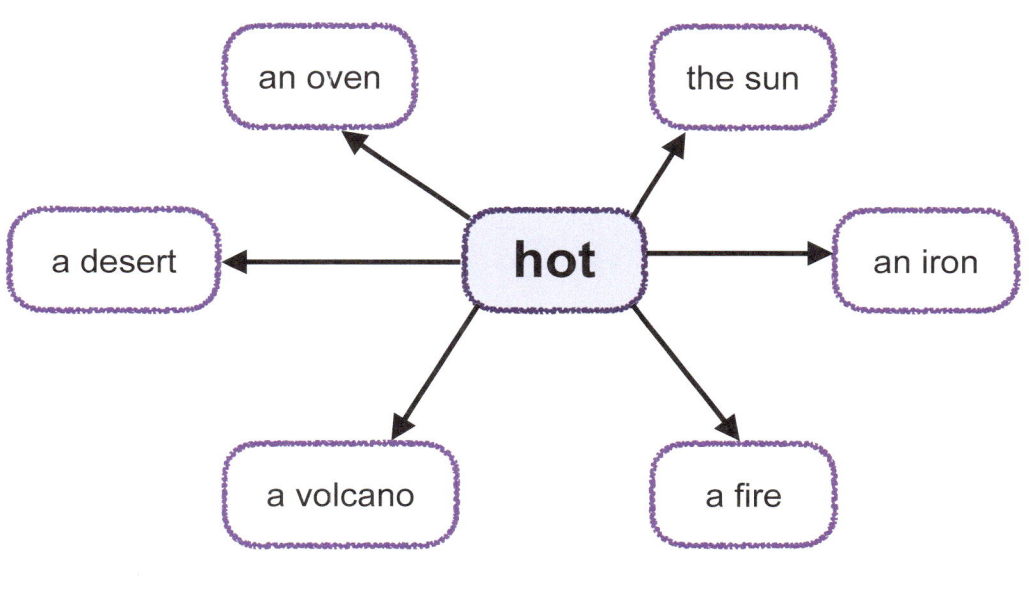

You can then use these ideas to create your simile:

as hot as a desert, as hot as an oven, as hot as the sun, as hot as an iron, as hot as a fire or as hot as a volcano.

hot like a desert, hot like an oven, hot like the sun, hot like an iron, hot like a fire or hot like a volcano.

Work together to collect ideas for similes for these words. Once you have collected your ideas try and write your similes.

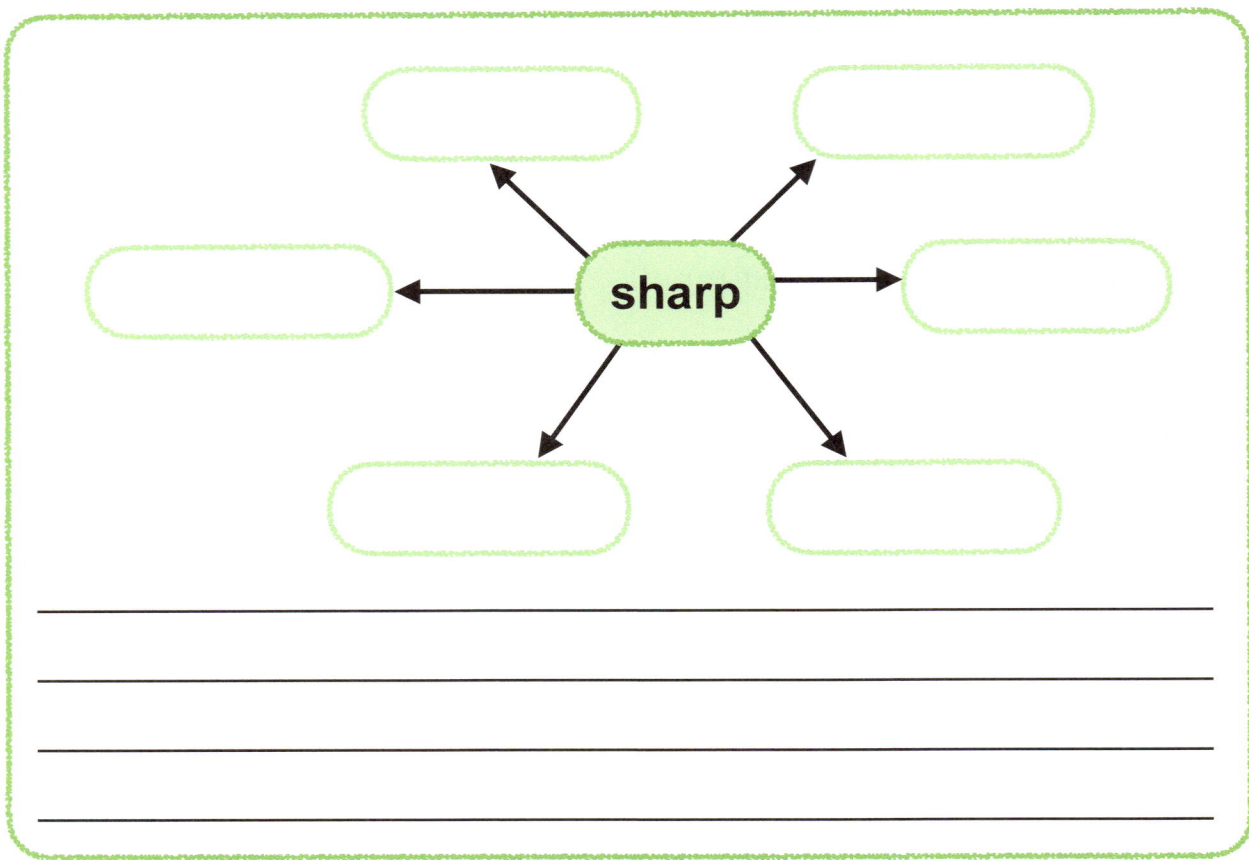

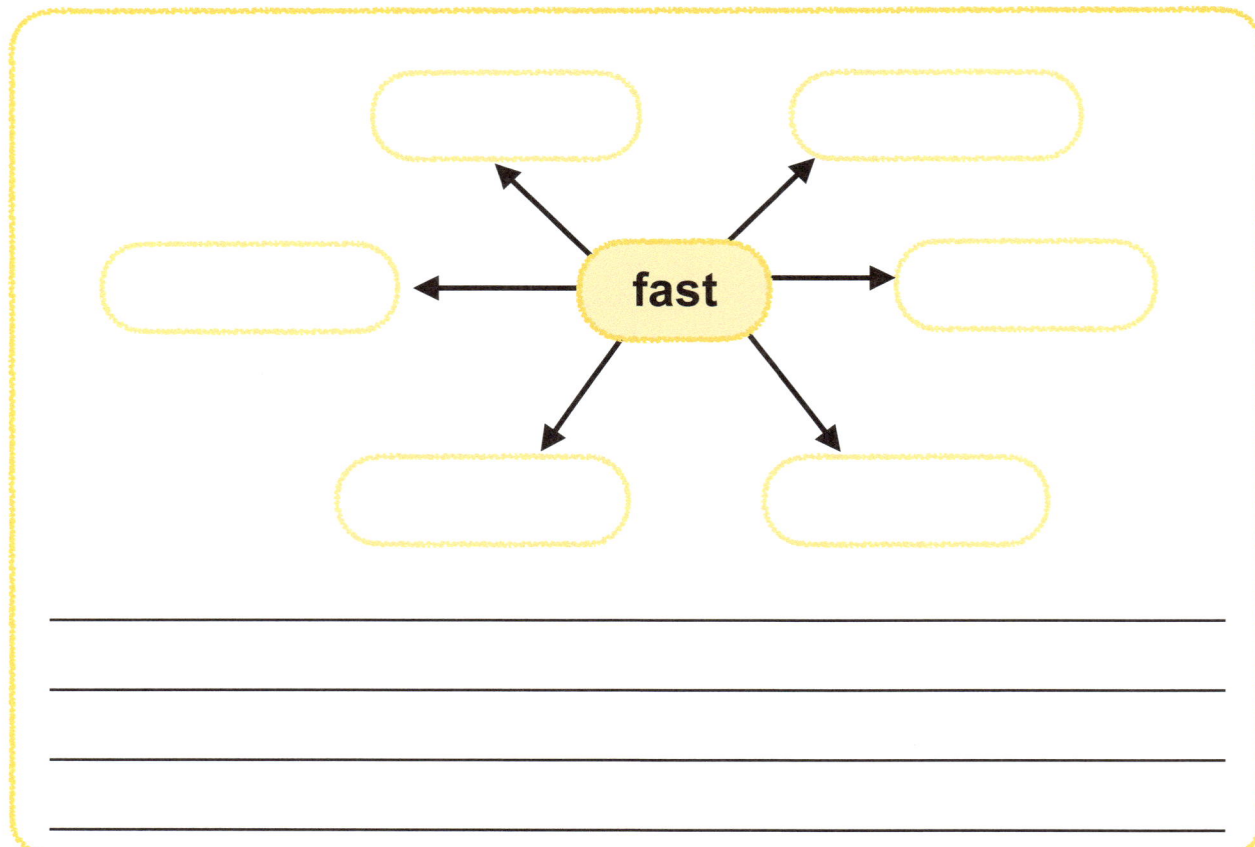

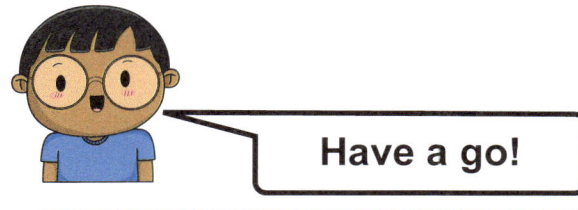

Have a go!

Underline the similes in the sentences below. Highlight the nouns that are being compared.

1. The roaring **fire** is as bright as the **sun**.
2. The freezer was as cold as an ice cube.
3. The water is cold like ice.
4. The doctor was as busy as a bee.
5. My mum is busy like a beaver.
6. The stars are as twinkly as diamonds.
7. The lights were bright like stars.
8. The car was speeding down the road as fast as a rocket.

Try writing your own similes - try to include different nouns for each of the similes.

as slow as
big like
as cold as
strong like
as smooth as
rough like
as dark as
loud like
as quiet as
tall like

13

Wrap it up!

Write some similes that could be used to describe the image below.

_____
_____
_____
_____
_____
_____
_____
_____
_____

Helen's helpful hint
Think carefully when you are writing your similes - remember that you are using them to help give your reader a clearer idea about what you are describing.

How to use onomatopoeia

Talk together!

Onomatopoeia is when a word makes the sound it describes.

Onomatopoeia could be:

animal noises	woof	roar	buzz	oink	tweet
human noises	groan	achoo	snort	sniff	boo
water sounds	splash	plop	trickle	gurgle	splish
collision sounds	crash	boom	bang	bump	smash
cooking sounds	sizzle	pop	crack	fizz	crunch

The sentences below use onomatopoeia. Notice, that the onomatopoeia acts as a **verb** in the sentence so sometimes has '**ing**' or '**ed**' at the end.

- Smash! The glass shattered as the stone hit it.
- The bees were buzzing as they flew from flower to flower.
- The engine spluttered as Fred tried to start his car.
- Boom! The thunder echoed through the sky.
- The brakes screeched as the car came to a sudden halt.

Helen's helpful hint

Sometimes we want to emphasise the onomatopoeia. We do this by adding an exclamation mark after it.

Gulp! Gulp! The giant gobbled the cake.
Bang! The door slammed shut.
"Ouch! That hurt!" yelled Ben.

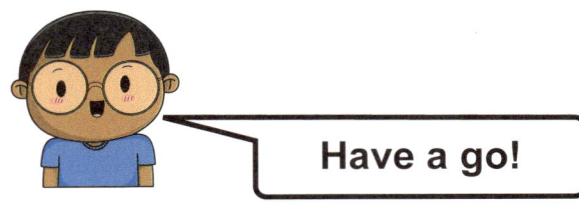

Have a go!

What onomatopoeia could you use in the situations below - can you think of more than one onomatopoeia word?

You fall over and hurt your knee.	
A cow on a farm.	
A police car driving	
A door being slammed close.	
Children playing a musical instrument.	
Taking a drink of juice.	
A doorbell	

Add an onomatopoeia to the sentence - use the word bank below to help you.

smash, bang, rumbled, snap, sizzling, thud, crashed, gurgles

1. I hit the ground with a _____.
2. The window broke with a loud _____.
3. The thunder _____ in the sky.
4. The water _____ down the drainpipe.
5. The branches _____ in the wind.
6. The waves _____ against the side of the ship.
7. The egg was _____ in the pan.
8. There was a loud _____ and everything went dark.

 Wrap it up!

 Amar says that he has underlined the onomatopoeia in his sentence.

Woof! The dogs were <u>barking</u> loudly.

Is he correct? Explain your answer.

_____
_____

 Kaylee says that she has underlined the onomatopoeia in her sentence.

The mouse went <u>squeak</u> as it ran across the room.

Is she correct? Explain your answer.

_____
_____

 Emily says that she has included an onomatopoeia in her sentence.

The plane flew quietly across the sky.

Is she correct? Explain your answer.

_____
_____

Creating alliteration effectively

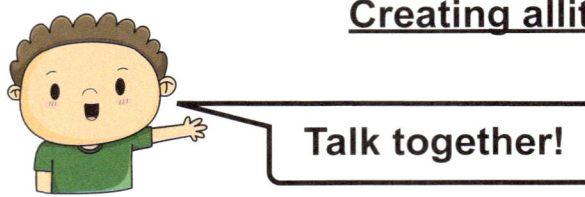

Talk together!

What is alliteration?

Alliteration is when the same sound is repeated at the beginning of several words in the same sentence. Alliteration is commonly found in tongue twisters and within poems. It can be used within stories to create dramatic effects.

What letter sound is repeated in this tongue twister?

She sells sea shells on the seashore.

How to create alliteration?

It is a good idea to build up word banks to help form alliteration.

If you wanted to create alliteration about a snake you would collect words that begin with an 's' sound. Include adjectives, adverbs and verbs in your list.

slither	slowly	silently	sliding	scary	smooth	soft
slips	seven	sneaky	sly	sleepy	scaly	secret

Once you have created a word bank, then begin creating your alliteration. Try not to make your alliteration too long - stick to a maximum of 4 words.

Begin to experiment with the word order:

- Seven snakes slither slowly
- The scary snake silently slithers by
- The snakes sneakily slither silently
- The sneaky snake sleepily slides

Have a go!

Make word banks for the following words:

Wizard

Mountains

Bees

Now use your word banks to create your alliteration.

Wizard

Mountains

Bees

Wrap it up!

Use what you have learned to help you write some alliteration about this image. You might find it helpful to annotate the image.

Introducing personification

Talk together!

What is personification?

Personification is when we give a human quality to an animal or non-human object.

The sun sang in the sky.

In the sentence above the **sun** (an object that isn't alive) has been personified by suggesting that it is doing an action that a human might do - **singing**.

How do we create personification?

When creating personification the first thing you need to do is decide what noun you want to personify.

In the next example, we will personify the **leaves**.

Once you have decided on the noun think about the verb that is going to be used with it.

You could use: **danced, swayed, hopped, cried or waved**.

Finally, add the personification to a sentence:

The **leaves danced** to the ground.
The **leaves swayed** in the breeze.
The **leaves hopped** off the branches.
The **leaves cried** as they were torn from the branches.
The **leaves waved** at the tree.

The verb choice will help to create the mood in your writing. Dancing, swaying and waving are creating happy moods but crying would create a sad mood.

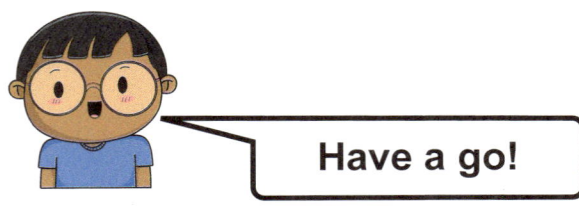

Have a go!

Circle the object or animal that is being personified. Underline the verb that forms the personification.

1. The (sun) <u>sang</u> in the sky.
2. My alarm clock yelled at me to get up.
3. The clouds danced across the sky.
4. The still water shivered in the wind.
5. The sky was full of dancing stars.
6. The snow whispered as it fell from the sky.
7. The car engine coughed in the cold morning.
8. The kettle whistled a joyful tune.
9. The waves gently tickled her toes as she stood on the shore.

Add a verb to the sentences to create your own personification.

1. The curtains _____ in the breeze.
2. The books _____ like soldiers on the bookshelf.
3. The last piece of pie was _____ my name.
4. The fire alarm was _____ at us to get out.
5. The stars _____ at each other in the night sky.
6. The leaves _____ in the gentle breeze.
7. The vines _____ themselves around the tree trunk.

Helen's helpful hint
Personification can help to create mood in your writing. It can be a happy mood or a gloomy/scary mood.

Look at the personification grid below and colour the happy mood in yellow and the gloomy/scary mood in blue.

The waves crashed against the boat.	The rays of the sun danced through the leaves.	The lightning smashed the city with its bolts.
The trees whispered in the breeze.	The waves gently stroked the shore.	The car's headlights glared at me.
The leaves waved in the wind.	The sun peered through the trees.	The waves angrily slapped the side of the ship.
Lightning danced across the sky.	Hailstones thumped against the window.	My alarm clock screamed at me to wake up.
The snowflakes pirouette in the sky.	The sun screamed in the sky.	The trees swayed in the wind.
The car's headlights winked at me.	The leaves danced in the wind.	The waves tickled her toes.
The flowers were begging for water.	The waves ran across the sand.	My warm coat hugged me.

Notice how changing the verb in the personification can change the mood. The verb **whispered** creates a **happier** mood than **yelled** or **screamed**.

Wrap it up!

Use what you have learned to help write some personification about this image. It might be helpful to annotate the image first.

_____
_____
_____
_____
_____
_____
_____
_____

Using body language to show feelings

Talk together!

When you write about a character you mustn't focus just on the way they look, also include their emotions. Ask yourself '**How is the character feeling?**'

To make your writing more interesting, include some body language to **show** how the character is feeling rather than just **telling** the reader the emotion. This is called '**show don't tell**'.

How do you think this character is feeling?
What clues are there in the image?
What is her mouth doing?
Look at her eyes, what do you notice?
What might the rest of her body be doing to show the emotion?

Compare the two paragraphs below:

James was really upset. He had short, curly brown hair and was wearing a new coat. He had fallen over and ripped his new coat.

Anya's face was as red as a beetroot, she wiped the tears from her eyes. Anya rubbed her knee as she hobbled across the room towards her mother's comforting arms.

Both of the paragraphs show that the character is upset because they have fallen over. Which do you find more interesting to read? Hopefully, you chose the second paragraph (the blue one) because it makes you (the reader) think a bit more about the character.

Underline the body language in the second paragraph above. What body language shows she is upset? What shows she is hurt? What other body language shows that someone is upset?

Have a go!

What body language could be used for the emotions below? First you will need to colour the emotion boxes.

excited	tired	sad / upset	nervous
angry/annoyed	shy	scared	happy

Now colour the body language boxes to match. Excited has been done for you as an example. Some boxes could be two colours.

wide eyes	crying / tears	looking down	butterflies in the tummy
shoulders slumped	red face	heart pounding	quiet
yawning	heart pounding	blowing nose	sparkling eyes
arms crossed	fiddling with hair	droopy eyes	clenched fists
goosebumps	jumping up and down	shouting	red eyes
legs shaking	standing alone	cover eyes	dragging feet
rosy cheeks	arms stretching	face beaming	face turns white
stomping	laughing	biting nails	waving arms

Helen's helpful hint
Verbs can also help to show the character's emotions. You could use the verb 'stamped' to show anger.

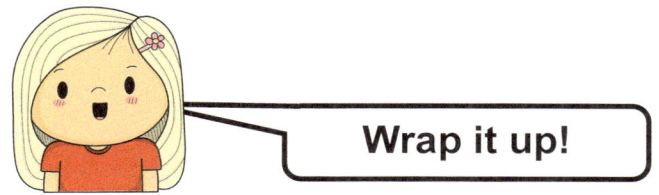

Wrap it up!

Using what you have learned about 'show don't tell' and body language, write a paragraph about these characters. Show their emotions through body language rather than just telling their emotions.

Using the senses

Talk together!

When you use the senses in your writing it helps to bring your characters to life and create a more vivid image in the reader's mind.

There are 5 senses that can be used in your writing:

- **Sight** (what can be seen)
- **Hearing** (what sounds can be heard)
- **Smell** (what scents can be smelled)
- **Taste** (the flavours of what is eaten)
- **Touch** (the description of how something feels)

Helen's helpful hint
When we use the senses in our writing it is sometimes referred to as '**imagery**'.

When writing stories it is often easy to focus on the **sights**:

- The character's **curly blonde hair**
- The **golden sand** on the beach
- The **long wooden fence** around the park

Although this adds description to your writing it doesn't use all of the senses.

When focusing on the character, you could mention the smell of their perfume or their high-pitched laugh rather than their appearance.

When writing about the beach, you could focus on the faint salty taste in the air or the squawking of the seagulls.

When describing a park, you could include the giggles of the children playing. If you wanted to focus on the fence you might use touch to describe the roughness of the wood.

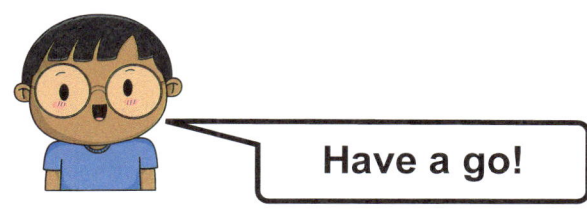

Have a go!

Look at the table below and colour the boxes to show which senses have been used. The first one has been done for you.

Sight	Hearing	Smell	Taste	Touch

The musty room	The tart lemons
The rough bark	The clattering plates
The luminous paint	The spicy curry
The pleasant aroma	The wailing baby
The spotty jumper	The prickly bush
The sodden blanket	The greasy sausages
The clear glass	The aromatic oils
The bland potatoes	The rustling leaves
The putrid smoke	The flashing lights
The smooth steel	The stench of rotten cabbage
The snarling dogs	The glowing eyes
The abrasive sandpaper	The appetising cakes
The pungent garlic	The chirping birds
The savoury biscuits	The dazzling lights
The creaking door	The gritty sand
The fragrant flowers	The jagged rocks

Wrap it up!

Look at the image below and add some sensory description to each of the boxes. You can include more than one idea in each box.

Sight

Hearing

Smell

Taste

Touch

What are clauses and phrases?

Talk together!

Clauses

A clause is a group of words that contain a **subject** and a **verb**.
I eat - I is the **subject**, eat is the **verb**. The subject is the noun that is doing the action.

Some clauses will have an **object** (another noun)
Jenny plays football. Jenny is the **subject**, plays is the **verb** and football is the **object**. The object is the noun that has the action done to it.

There could also be an **adverb**.
Paul sings happily. Paul is the **subject**, sings is the **verb** and happily is the **adverb**. In this case, an adverb of manner has been used to show how Paul is singing.

The clauses that we have looked at so far are **main clauses** (these are also called **independent clauses**) they make complete sentences on their own.

The other type of clause we are going to look at is a **subordinate clause** (these are sometimes called **dependent clauses**).

After I wake up - this is a **subordinate clause** because it doesn't make complete sense without a **main clause**.

After I wake up, I greedily eat sausages. Once the **main clause** is added the **subordinate clause** makes sense.

The subordinate clause can go either at the beginning or at the end of the sentence. **I greedily eat sausages after I wake up.**

Phrases

A phrase is 2 or more words that give extra meaning to clauses. A phrase **does not contain a verb**. Phrases do not make complete sense on their own - they rely on the information in the main clause.

There are several types of phrases:

Expanded noun phrases - these give more details about the noun. In a sentence, the expanded noun phrase acts as a noun.

Prepositional phrases - these always begin with a preposition and can act as either an adjective or adverb. Prepositional phrases are always either **adverbial phrases** or **adjective phrases**.

Adverbial phrases - these add more details to the verb or adjective - they work in the same way as an adverb.

Adjective phrases - these give more information about nouns or pronouns - they act as an adjective in the sentence.

The boy **in the green jumper** was playing football. 'In the green jumper' is the **prepositional phrase** beginning with the preposition '**in**'. It is also an **adjective phrase** as it tells us more about the boy.

In the morning, I am going to school. 'In the morning' is a **prepositional phrase** that is also an **adverbial phrase** as it tells the reader more about when the verb is happening.

I go to work **on the bus**. 'On the bus' is a **prepositional phrase**. It is also an **adverbial phrase** as it explains how I go to work.

The boy wore **a thick, woollen jumper**. 'A thick woollen jumper' is an **expanded noun phrase** as it gives more information about the noun (the jumper).

Yesterday morning, I went to the supermarket to buy **some freshly-baked bread**. This sentence contains two phrases. 'Yesterday morning' is an **adverbial phrase** telling when the action was happening. 'Some freshly-baked bread' is an **expanded noun phrase.**

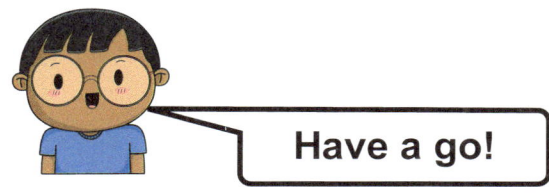

Have a go!

Look at the sentences below. Decide if the underlined words are phrases or clauses. Work out what type of phrase or clause is being used.

	phrase	clause
I went to the park **on Tuesday afternoon**.		
The dog sat on the mat in the garden.		
The children run **around the park**.		
We are visiting the castle near the park.		
The cheerful lady works **in the office**.		
The children watched television **after they had eaten their dinner.**		
The grumpy, old man slipped down the stairs.		
The fox was hiding in the thick, prickly hedge.		
On the brightly lit stage, the boy began to play the guitar.		
Bursting into tears, **the boy ran** towards his home.		
I gave my mum **a beautiful, antique ring**.		

Wrap it up!

Add a phrase to these main clauses. The first one has been done for you.

1. We played football.
   We played football **in the park.**

2. James watched the television.
   _____

3. Fatima ate her dinner.
   _____

4. The boy hid.
   _____

5. The boy wore a jumper.
   _____

Helen's helpful hint
A phrase can be within a clause but a phrase can not have a clause within it.

Underline the prepositional phrases in the sentences - are they acting as adjectives or adverbs? The first one has been for you.

1. We are going to the zoo <u>on Thursday.</u>
2. The boy hid under the bed when playing hide and seek.
3. I peered through the window to see the birds.
4. Sam put the heavy box on the table.
5. At the weekend, Henry watched a film.
6. The lazy dog slept in its bed.

The three types of sentence structures

Talk together!

In English, there are three types of sentences: **simple**, **compound** and **complex**.
A **simple sentence** is made up of one main (independent) clause.
A **compound sentence** is made up of two or more main clauses and a coordinating conjunction.
A **complex sentence** is one main clause and a subordinate clause that begins with a subordinating conjunction.

To create a **compound sentence** you use a **coordinating conjunction** to join the main clauses. There are seven coordinating conjunctions.

for	and	nor	but	or	yet	so

Look at how these two main clauses can be joined:

Jane was hungry. She ate a cheese and tomato pizza.
Jane was hungry **so** she ate a cheese and tomato pizza.

The conjunction '**so**' has been used to create a **compound sentence**.

When creating **complex sentences** we use **subordinating** conjunctions. Here are some of the common ones.

before	after	when	while	until
once	because	since	as	if

To create a complex sentence a subordinate clause is added to a main clause. The subordinate clause is a dependent clause so doesn't make complete sense on its own - it needs the main clause.

I went to the park because the sun was shining.

Main clause   **subordinating conjunction**   **subordinate clause**

Have a go!

Look at the sentences below. Decide what type of sentence they are.

	simple	compound	complex
Paul was tired so he went to bed.			
Tomorrow, I am going on holiday.			
After he has completed his homework, he will watch the television.			
I wanted to swim in the sea but the water was too cold.			
The boy wore a dirty jumper.			
Harry turned off his light and went to sleep.			
Before the film began, the children ate their popcorn.			
Mick was playing on the computer.			
The old man slipped over because it was icy outside.			
Before we went to the shops, we made a list of what to buy.			
I lost the key to the front door.			
I lost the key to the front door so I couldn't get in.			

Wrap it up!

Write some sentences about the image below. Try to include simple compound and complex sentences. Include phrases in some of your sentences.

Using a 'where' sentence starter

Talk together!

A **where** sentence starter tells the reader more about where the action is taking place. It begins with a **prepositional phrase** that acts as an **adverbial of place** - these are often referred to as **fronted adverbials**. When writing this type of sentence the adverbial goes at the beginning of the sentence and is **followed by a comma**.

Here are some examples of adverbials of place that can be used in your sentences. You can change them to make them your own, for example, you can change the noun to make a different adverbial - **under the bed** instead of **under the sea**.

A long way from here,	On top of the mountain,
In the silver box,	Under the water,
Outside of the gates,	Across the room,
Behind the door,	Out of the way,
Beyond the village,	In the distance,
On the corner of the street,	Over there,
Down by the seashore,	Behind the bushes,
Under the sea,	Beneath the waves,
Over the hills,	Inside the house,
East of the river,	To the north of the town,
Along the dirt track,	Near the swimming pool,
Ahead of the group,	Somewhere close by,

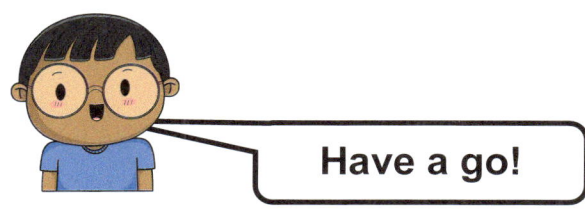

Have a go!

Underline the **where** starter (adverbial of place) and add the comma to these sentences.

1. On top of the hill there stood three exhausted figures.
2. Beneath the water the fish swum happily.
3. Behind the tree a little boy crouched silently.
4. Under the bed the boy frantically searched for his torch.
5. Beyond the town there stood an ancient castle.
6. Near the supermarket an old lady sat on a bench.

Underline the adverbial of place and rewrite the sentence with the adverbial at the beginning of the sentence. You need to remember to add a comma after the adverbial.

1. The children sat in silence <u>in the classroom</u>.
   <u>In the classroom,</u> the children sat in silence.

2. A cloaked figure appeared from behind the building.

   _____

3. The group of children waited outside the gates.

   _____

4. Mary sat happily building a sandcastle on the beach.

   _____

5. A loud scream echoed from behind the door.

   _____

6. The dog was frantically barking on the other side of the wall.

   _____

Wrap it up!

Helen's helpful hint
Remember to add the comma after the adverbial of place.

Add a suitable adverbial of place before these main clauses.

1. _____ the boys were playing football.
2. _____ the birds sang sweetly.
3. _____ Sam ate a strawberry lolly.
4. _____ Jack was building sandcastles.
5. _____ I could see the mountain peaks.
6. _____ the children were making a plan.
7. _____ the footballer aimed for the goal.

Add a suitable main clause after these adverbials of place.

1. In the distance
_____

2. Down by the river
_____

3. In the water
_____

4. Somewhere close by
_____

40

Using a 'when' sentence starter

Talk together!

A **when** sentence starter tells the reader more about when the action is taking place. It begins with a **prepositional phrase** that acts as an **adverbial of time** - these are often called **fronted adverbials**. When writing this type of sentence the adverbial goes at the beginning of the sentence and is **followed by a comma**.

Here are some examples of adverbials of time that can be used in your sentences. You can change them to make them your own, for example, you can change the noun to make a different adverbial - **in February** instead of **in March.**

In March,	In the morning,
At midnight,	At 1 o'clock,
On Friday,	In the middle of summer,
Late one afternoon,	Early in the morning,
Immediately,	Yesterday,
Tomorrow,	Eventually,
Just then,	Soon,
Last week,	As soon as he could,
Later that day,	Afterwards,
All of a sudden,	After a while,
Every Wednesday,	After breakfast,
Every day,	Later that afternoon,

Have a go!

Underline the adverbial of time. Add a comma after it so that it is separated from the rest of the sentence.

1. In the middle of the night a strange sound could be heard outside.
2. All of a sudden the door swung open.
3. Last year Jack went on holiday to Spain.
4. In the autumn the leaves fall off of the trees.
5. As soon as possible he leapt from the speeding car.
6. In the blink of an eye it finished.

Underline the adverbial of time and rewrite the sentence with the adverbial at the beginning of the sentence. You need to remember to add a comma after the adverbial.

1. The children sat in the assembly hall <u>in the morning.</u>
   <u>In the morning,</u> the children sat in the assembly hall.

2. The boys enjoyed playing football in the park on Saturday.
   _____

3. The children went to the beach in the summer holidays.
   _____

4. There was a loud bang in the middle of the night.
   _____

5. The children crept out of their beds early in the morning.
   _____

6. Mary went for a walk in the park late in the afternoon.
   _____

Wrap it up!

Add a suitable adverbial of time before these main clauses.

1. _____ the girls watched a film.
2. _____ the dog howled loudly.
3. _____ Fred was eating his tea.
4. _____ a dark figure appeared.
5. _____ I walked to the shops.
6. _____ I celebrated my birthday.
7. _____ it was dark.

Helen's helpful hint
Remember to add the comma after the adverbial of time.

Add a suitable main clause after these adverbials of time.

1. At midnight _____
   _____

2. On Thursday morning _____
   _____

3. In the middle of winter _____
   _____

4. Later in the afternoon _____
   _____

Using an 'emotion word' starter

Talk together!

This type of sentence begins with an **emotion adjective** (not an adverb) that tells the reader more about how the character is feeling.

There is a **comma** after the **emotion adjective** separating it from the rest of the sentence. This type of sentence usually has the character's name or a personal pronoun as the first word after the comma.

Emotion word starters are used to help the reader focus on the character's emotions rather than what they are doing. You could link this sentence type with the body language you learned earlier.

It is important that the sentence makes complete sense even if the emotion word isn't there.

Excited, she skipped across the park.

The sentence above would still make sense without excited at the beginning.

Here are some example sentences. There is a list of emotion words that could be used on page 99.

Petrified, Sam screamed for help.
Terrified, she curled into a ball.
Anxious, the figure moved slowly towards him.
Concerned, she looked over her shoulder.
Dismayed, he didn't know what to do next.
Ashamed, he hid his face from his friends.
Livid, Paul yelled at the top of his voice.
Stumped, Alex thought about what he should do.
Distressed, Holly wiped away her tears.

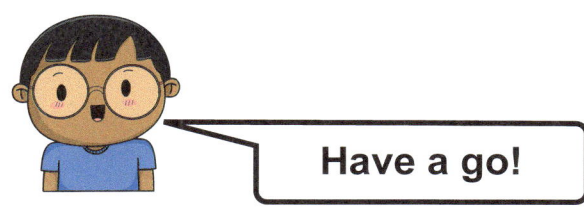

Have a go!

Add a suitable emotion adjective to the beginning of these sentences. Remember that you need to add a comma after the emotion.

1. _With Fear_ Hannah ran as fast as she could.
2. _With excitement_ Nivi ripped open his present.
3. _With anger_ Eloise shouted at her younger sister.
4. _With happiness_ Ryan kicked the ball to the back of the goal.
5. _Afraid_ Anya hid under her bed.
6. _With confusion_ Nathan stared at the figure in front of him.

Helen's helpful hint
Remember, the sentence needs to make complete sense without the emotion adjective at the beginning.

Complete the sentences. Think carefully about what might come after the emotion word.

1. Confused _____
2. Horrified _____
3. Furious _____
4. Delighted _____
5. Infuriated _____
6. Nervous _____
7. Startled _____
8. Jubilant _____

Wrap it up!

Emily says that she has underlined the emotion word starter in her sentence.

Delighted, he <u>ripped</u> open the envelope.

Is she correct? Explain your answer.

_____
_____

Kaylee says that she has used an emotion word starter in her sentence.

On Tuesday, I went to the dentist.

Is she correct? Explain your answer.

_____
_____

Sam says that he has included a suitable emotion word starter for his sentence.

Terrified, she skipped across the playground.

Is he correct? Explain your answer.

_____
_____

Using an 'ing' sentence starter

Talk together!

When you begin your sentences with an 'ing' word you are focusing on the actions of the character. If used correctly, these sentence structures can add variety to your writing.

Two rules need to be followed when using this structure:

- You need to **add a comma** after the introductory group of words (this might be just the 'ing' word or the 'ing' word and some other words).
- You need to say **who** or **what** is doing the 'ing' word within a few words of the comma.

Trembling with fear, **Luke** hid from the mysterious figure.

In the sentence above **trembling** is the 'ing' word but the comma follows the word fear as **with fear** is the way that Luke is trembling. **Luke** is the one **who** is trembling.

Here are some 'ing' starters for you to use. Remember, like the **where** and **when** starters you can change the words after the 'ing' word to make them fit your story.

Grabbing her bag,	Driving down the road,
Looking behind her,	Searching for the exit,
Holding his breath,	Flashing in the distance,
Dreading the answer,	Chasing her enemy,
Noticing a movement,	Plodding along the path.
Heading out of the door,	Waving frantically,
Shivering in the wind,	Lurking in the woods,
Breathing heavily,	Crying in pain,
Enjoying the film,	Feeling exhausted,

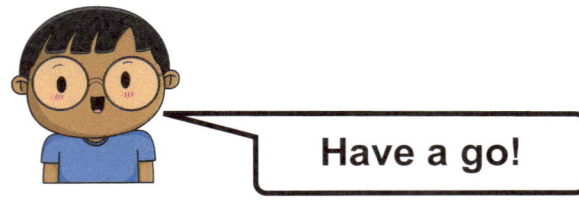

Have a go!

Look at the sentences below. Underline the 'ing' word and the 'who' then add the comma after the opener. The first one has been done for you.

1. <u>**Gazing**</u> out of the window, <u>**Harry**</u> saw two cars collide.
2. Drawing his sword the knight went into battle.
3. Noticing the commotion the children ran to see what was going on outside.
4. Feeling tired Dave fell asleep at the cinema.
5. Sprinting quickly Anna grabbed the prize.
6. Wailing in pain Steven limped towards the door.
7. Leaping into the water Jack made a huge splash.
8. Moving quickly they could sense the danger ahead.
9. Staring into space she had lost track of time.
10. Listening carefully to the instructions James completed the task.

Add a main clause after the 'ing' starter. Remember that you need to include a comma after the sentence starter. You also need to add a **who** to show who is doing the action.

1. Screaming in pain
2. Breathing heavily
3. Feeling excited
4. Moving quickly
5. Lurking in the darkness
6. Looking behind her
7. Treading carefully
8. Scrambling through the bushes

 Wrap it up!

Emily says that she has used an 'ing' sentence starter.

In the morning, Harry was watching a film.

Is she correct? Explain your answer.

_____
_____

Add a suitable 'ing' starter to Amar's sentence.

_____ **the man sprinted down the road.**

Make sure you have included all of the punctuation.

Sam says that he has used a suitable 'ing' starter for his sentence.

Screaming in pain, Zoe happily bounded to the park.

Is he correct? Explain your answer.

_____
_____

Using an 'adverb of manner' starter

Talk together!

This sentence starter, uses '**adverbs of manner**' that end in '**ly**'. By doing this, you are giving the reader more information about the verb in the main clause.

You can use a single adverb followed by a comma - **Quietly,** she sneaked along the hallway. **Quietly** is the **adverb** showing how she is sneaking.

You could use two adverbs at the beginning of the sentence. **Quietly** and **carefully,** she sneaked along the hallway. If you use this sentence structure both of the adverbs need to show how the verb is being done.

There is a list of adverbs of manner on page 100.

Here is another way that '**adverbs of manner**' can be used to begin sentences. The sentence starter is still separated from the main clause with a comma.

Cautiously creeping through the tunnel,	Gradually appearing through the trees,
Swiftly sprinting for help,	Perfectly warm and cosy,
Desperately searching for food,	Strikingly beautiful,
Exhaustedly bashing on the door,	Silently moving through the dark night,
Excitedly ripping the paper,	Noisily crunching his crisps,
Proudly watching the performance,	Painfully limping with her wooden crutches,
Furiously screaming at the children,	Athletically sprinting towards the finish line,
Miserably packing her bag,	Carefully avoiding the potholes,

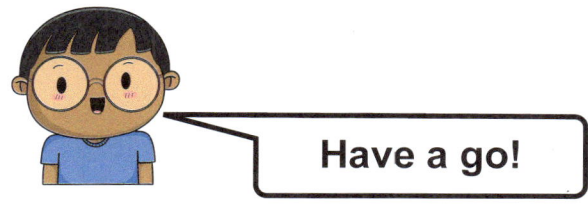

Have a go!

Look at the sentences below. Underline the adverb of manner starter and add the comma in the correct place. The first one has been done for you.

1. **<u>Angrily,</u>** she stormed upstairs to her bedroom.
2. Victoriously and enthusiastically, Ella sprinted over the finish line.
3. Aggressively waving his sword, the knight charged.
4. Nervously walking towards the door, Jim looked to see if anyone was around.
5. Unexpectedly, a huge dog hurtled towards the children.
6. Recklessly and defiantly, he sped through the red light.
7. Gleefully and joyfully, Molly skipped along the road.
8. Ridiculously lost and not knowing where to turn, Adam finally got out the map.

Add a suitable main clause to the adverb of manner starter. Remember to include a comma.

1. Calmly working out what to do next

   _____

2. Bravely and reassuringly

   _____

3. Energetically

   _____

4. Frustratedly looking at his watch

   _____

5. Suspiciously

   _____

Wrap it up!

Kaylee says that she has used an adverb of manner sentence starter.

Yesterday, Karen went to the park.

Is she correct? Explain your answer.

_____
_____

Add a suitable adverb of manner starter to Emily's sentence

_____ **the man crept through the door.**

Make sure you have included all of the punctuation.

Amar says that he has used a suitable adverb of manner sentence starter.

Fiercely, the lady smiled at James.

Is he correct? Explain your answer.

_____
_____

How to structure your writing into paragraphs

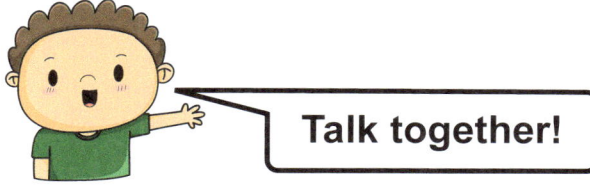

Talk together!

When writing a story it needs to be written in paragraphs. To be able to do this you need to know what a paragraph is and when you should begin a new one.

What is a paragraph?

A paragraph is a group of sentences that are written about one idea or topic. They help to structure your writing so that it is not one long block of writing. They make your stories easier for the reader to read.

To show that you are starting a new paragraph begin a new line. You need to miss a line between paragraphs, this makes it clearer for the reader to see where the new paragraph begins.

When to start a new paragraph.

Use the **TiP ToP** rule to help you to decide if you need to begin a new paragraph. You must follow these rules when writing your stories.

Time	If you change the **time** in your story you to need a new paragraph.
Place	If you change **place** in your story you need a new paragraph.
Topic	If you start to write about a new **topic** (**idea**) you need a new paragraph.
Person	If you introduce a new **person** (**character**) you need a new paragraph.

There is no set number for how many sentences need to be in a paragraph. Some are short and only have 3-4 sentences; others can be 10 or more sentences.

When writing paragraphs they need to be structured in a logical order. This means that you need to think about the order of the events in your stories.

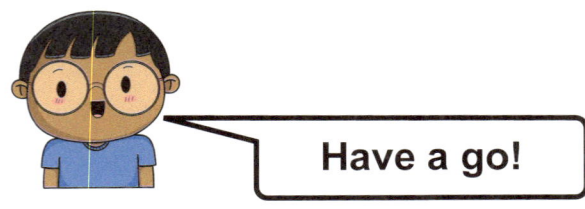

Have a go!

Read the paragraph below:

Steve stomped across the room, his heart was pounding. He loved to eat ice-cream. He muttered something about a barking dog under his breath. Woof! Woof! Woof! Came the noise from outside his door.

Underline the sentence that doesn't belong in the paragraph. Why does it not belong?
_____

Read the paragraph below:

She quickly rushed to the bathroom and brushed her teeth. Sally lazily got out of bed. She hurried downstairs and grabbed her bag before heading out the door.

Is it written in the correct order? Rewrite it below so that it is in the correct order.
_____
_____
_____
_____
_____
_____
_____
_____
_____

Wrap it up!

Helen's helpful hint
Remember that when beginning a new paragraph you need to miss a line.

Read the paragraph below:

Harry and Max were exhausted, they had been kicking the ball around the park all afternoon. They hurriedly snatched their bags and headed towards the shop. When they arrived at the shop, they dashed towards the fridge. Excitedly, they grabbed an ice-cold bottle of drink to quench their thirst.

Split it into 2 paragraphs. Add in some literary devices to make the paragraphs more interesting.

_____
_____
_____
_____
_____
_____
_____
_____
_____
_____
_____
_____
_____

How to introduce your setting

Talk together!

When introducing the setting in your story try to include vivid descriptions so that the reader has a clear image in their head. Include the senses - you learned about this on page 28. Try and include the overall atmosphere of the place.

You need to answer the questions **where** and **when**.

Read these two setting descriptions. Which is more effective? Why?

It was early morning and Paul was standing at the top of the mountain. He was feeling cold.

The sun began to rise above the majestic mountains. Paul took a deep breath, breathing in the crisp morning air. In the distance, he could hear the faint chirping of the birds welcoming a new day. He stood awestruck, taking in the breathtaking panoramic view. The jagged rocks reached up and poked through the clouds that were scattered across the sky. A gentle breeze tickled his cheeks as he took his first step on the soft mossy carpet.

I hope you will have decided that the second setting description was more effective because it creates a clearer picture in the reader's mind. They know where the story is **set**, and what **time of day** it is. There are a range of **literary devices** and it includes details that mention **the senses**. When you read the second opening it gives the idea of quite a calm and relaxing environment.

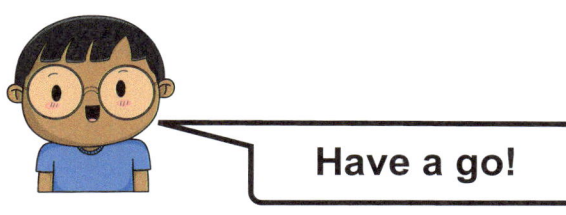

Have a go!

Use what you have learned about introducing the setting to improve these boring setting descriptions.

It was lunchtime and the children were playing on the playground. They were enjoying the games.

_____
_____
_____
_____
_____

It was early morning and mum was at the market looking at the fruit and vegetables.

_____
_____
_____
_____
_____
_____
_____

Helen's helpful hint
Remember to try and include all of the senses to give the reader a clearer image in their mind.

Wrap it up!

Write a setting description for this image. You might want to include a character but remember to focus on the setting. Try to include the literary devices you have learned so far.

| Simile |
| Alliteration |
| Onomatopoeia |
| Personification |
| The senses |

How to introduce a character

Talk together!

The word '**character**' refers to the person in your story. When you start to create a character ask yourself these questions:

- **What** is their name?
- **Where** are they?
- **What** do they look like?
- **How** do they behave?
- **What** do they enjoy doing?
- **What** do they dislike?

Once you have done this you will have a clearer idea about your overall character.

When introducing a character into a story you need to think about more than their appearance.

- Include the character's **personality** and what they are like as a person.
- Include what the character **might do** and **how they will act**.
- Include the character's **thoughts and feelings**.
- Include the **body language** that the character might show.
- Include the **name** of the character as it helps to bring them to life.
- Include **dialogue** - think about what your character might say.

The description below focuses a lot on the girl's appearance. It doesn't tell the reader what they are like as a person.

> The little girl was 7 years old. She had curly, blonde hair and was wearing a pink, flowery dress. She has blue, sparkling eyes. She was wearing a new pair of shiny black shoes.

This description tells the reader more about the character, where she is and what she is doing.

> Jasmine happily skipped across the playground, her blue eyes sparkling in the sunlight. She excitedly approached the swings. Enthusiastically, Jasmine screeched with delight at the sight of her friends running towards her.

Have a go!

Look at the character above and answer the questions about them. Use your imagination.

- What is their name?
- How old are they?
- What do they look like?
- What is their personality?
- Where are they?
- What are they doing?
- How are they feeling?

Once you have done this you will have a clearer idea about your overall character. Write a paragraph introducing your character.

Wrap it up!

Helen's helpful hint
When writing about your character write in the third person (use the pronouns he/she/they).

Using what you have learned, write a paragraph introducing the character below. Before you start writing, ask yourself questions about the character.

Name
Thoughts
Feelings
Actions
Personality

___

How to plan your writing

Talk together!

There are many things that you need to think about when planning and writing a short story. The first things to think about are who is the character (who is going to be in the story) and where is the setting (where is the story going to take place). Once you have thought about this you will then be able to think about the plot.

The plot

The plot is what will happen in the story. When planning short stories there are 5 key parts:

- **The opening** (introduces the character and setting)
- **The build-up** (the story gets going)
- **The problem** (something goes wrong)
- **The solution** (the problem is solved)
- **The ending**

In this book, we are going to focus on the **opening**, **problem** and **solution** sections of a story.

The language

Once you have a rough idea of the plot, begin to think about the different literary devices that could be used within the story. Use word mats, vocabulary walls, thesaurus or other language charts to help you collect ideas. At this stage, your ideas do not need to be in complete sentences - they will be structured once you begin writing your story.

Helen's helpful hint
This is the most important stage of story writing. It is when you collect all of your ideas before you start writing.

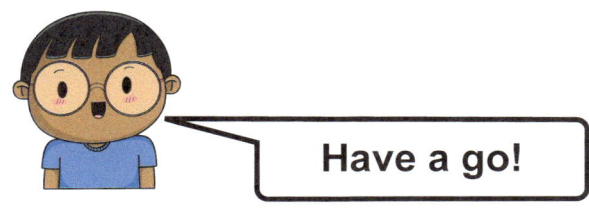

Have a go!

Look at the grid below. Colour the boxes to show if the ideas are from the opening, the problem or the solution part of the story. The first one has been done for you.

The opening	The problem	The solution
The fire brigade put the fire out.	The children went to the seaside.	There was a cheeky boy called Tom playing by a lake.
The volcano erupted.	The driver manages to press the brakes.	Lisa was in a boat on the sea.
A family go out for a drive.	The family left and went to a safe place.	The house caught fire.
The boy fell into the lake.	Max was in the bedroom playing with matches.	A passer-by sees a boy in the lake and pulls him out.
The children got lost on the beach and couldn't find their parents.	She climbs on the rocks to get to somewhere safe.	A family went on holiday to Italy to visit a volcano.
The car speeds towards the cliff edge.	Their parents found them and they went for an ice cream.	The boat crashes into the rocks.

Now see if you can work out which openings, problems and solutions belong together.

Example:
- Max was in the bedroom playing with matches. (opening)
- The house caught fire. (problem)
- The fire brigade came and put the fire out. (solution)

Talk together!

Once you have thought about the plot, you need to think about the language you could use in your story. Below is a sample plot that shows the language that could be used in the story. When thinking about the language, you don't need to write your ideas in complete sentences. Try to include a range of literary devices, sentence starters and some dialogue on your plan, this will help to make it easier when writing the story.

The opening	The problem	The solution
Plot Max was in the bedroom playing with matches.	The house caught fire	The fire brigade came and put the fire out.
Language Late in the afternoon, a cheerful, young boy Excitedly, Playing happily, mischievous Max fiddled with the matches the matches were calling his eyes widened	as hot as the sun crackling flames the rancid smell of smoke filled the air flames ran up the curtains "Help!" screamed Max at the top of his voice. the raging fire coughing and spluttering flames flickering furiously Crash!	Terrified, the screaming siren of the fire engine Trembling with fear, Courageously, ruby red fire engine whooshing water as loud as thunder friendly fireman fought Gasping for air, Splash!

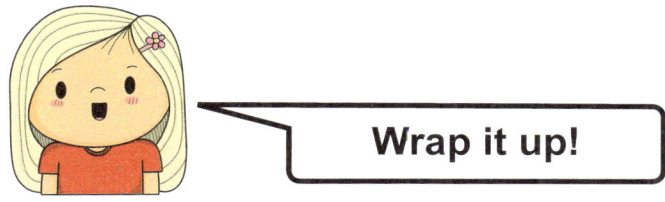

Wrap it up!

Use one of the other plots in the 'have a go!' section on page 63 and add your own language to it.

The opening	The problem	The solution
Plot		
Language		

How to write your opening

Talk together!

The opening is at the beginning of your story, it needs to grab the reader's attention and make them want to read on.

The purpose of the opening of your story is to introduce the main character and the setting. This part of your story might need to be more than one paragraph.

There are several ways that you can begin your story. You can use a **description opening** where the setting is introduced before the character. This type of opening is used to create an **atmosphere**, it works particularly well when the **senses** are included.

> Cobwebs clung to the broken window pane. Crackle! The lightning lit up the gloomy night sky. The thunder roared in the distance. The musty earth filled the air following the downpour. The ancient house had stood deserted for many years. Not a soul dared to visit - not until now!

If you use this type of opener, you will need a second paragraph to introduce the character.

You could use a **character opening**. This is where you focus more on what the character is doing and give the reader a few clues about the setting. This opening works well if you focus on the **actions of the character** rather than their appearance.

> Suzie's heart pounded as she cautiously crept towards the dilapidated building at the top of the hill. "Be brave," she muttered to herself. Wrapping her thick, red coat tighter around her chest, she continued up the hill.

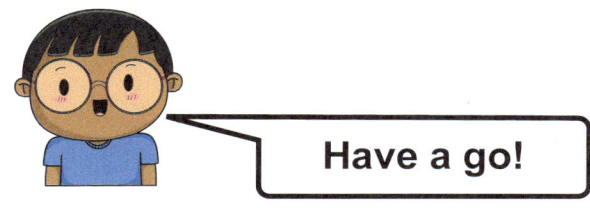

Have a go!

Use what you have learned about story openings to write a character opening and a description opening.

> It was late afternoon and Harry was playing with his toys in his bedroom.

___

> It was pouring with rain as they headed towards the mountains.

___

Wrap it up!

Write a story opener using this image. Decide if you want to write a character opening or a description opening. Try to include the literary devices you have learned so far.

Simile
Alliteration
Onomatopoeia
Personification
The senses

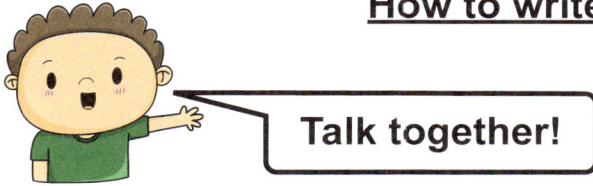

How to write your problem

Talk together!

In the problem section of a story, something bad often happens to the main character. It is in this section of the story that you need to try and create **tension** and **suspense**.

Tension means creating fear and worry for the main character.

Suspense is when the characters are waiting for something scary or mysterious to happen.

How can you create tension and suspense?

- Include some **description** of the surroundings so that the reader has a clear picture in their mind.
- Don't tell the reader everything at the beginning of the problem section - keep the reader waiting by **giving them clues**.
- Use **short sentences** with a maximum of 5 words to shock the reader a bit.
- Give the reader some **extra information** by using complex sentences - this makes the reader wait longer.
- Use **body language** rather than the character's emotions. A shiver ran down her spine is more effective than she was scared.
- Include all of **the senses**. The smells and sounds can be just as scary as the sights.
- Include **synonyms** of verbs. By using the verb crept instead of walked you are creating more suspense.
- Include a **rhetorical question** to make the reader think about what might happen next.
- Use the **weather/time of day** to create suspense. Have you noticed how scary stories are often set in darkness or fog?
- Include **onomatopoeia** and **similes** - these literary devices can help you create tension.
- Use **ellipses** (...) to add a dramatic pause - this makes the reader wonder what will happen next. (Only use ellipses occasionally.)

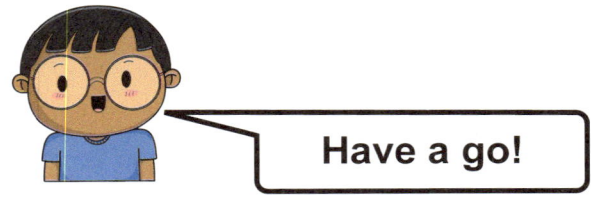

Have a go!

Look at the problem paragraphs below and underline the features. First, you will need to decide what colours you are going to use. The first one has been done for you. Some of the words will be more than one colour.

Description of surroundings	Clues	Short sentences	Longer complex sentences
Body language	Includes the senses	Synonyms	Rhetorical question
Ellipses	Include the weather	Onomatopoeia	Similes

Max looked... What had he done? The rancid smell of smoke started to fill the air causing him to wheeze. He drew a breath. The thick fumes tickled his nose and filled his lungs.

Slowly, with dread filling his body, he edged towards the bedroom door. As the crackling flames roared louder engulfing the room, Max began to tremble. His palms were clammy. How would he escape?

"Help!" screamed Max at the top of his voice. The raging flames as hot as the sun ran up the curtains. Sweat ran down his face. Smash! The window cracked into a million pieces. The cold night air blew into the bedroom sending the red-hot flames shooting towards Max. Would help arrive in time?

Wrap it up!

Write the problem section for a story about a ship in the storm. Try to include the features you have learned in this section.

Description	The senses
Give clues	Synonyms
Short sentences	Rhetorical question
Longer sentences	Onomatopoeia/ simile
Body language	Ellipses

How to write your solution

Talk together!

The solution section of your story is when the character **solves the problem**. This section comes just before the end of your story. You might need more than one paragraph in this section. The **solution** section of the story **needs to be linked** to the **problem**.

If you don't have a solution in your story the reader will be left wondering about the outcome and might be confused.

The solution needs to be **interesting** and **keep the reader wondering** if the problem will be solved.

When you write your solution think about how the character solves the problem. It is often good at this point to include some **dialogue** (speech) to show that the character is reflecting on the problem.

"I knew we should have stayed on the path," muttered Alex as he looked closely at the map.

In the solution think about how the character has changed in the story. What have they learned? Think about how the character feels about solving the problem.

Try to include the following features in your solution:
- A range of **sentence starters** - to keep the writing interesting.
- **Synonyms of verbs** - to give the reader a clearer image of what the character is doing.
- **Alliteration** - to create mood or give an emotive effect.
- **Smilies** - to help the reader understand more clearly.
- **Body language** - to show the way the character is feeling.
- Include **dialogue** - to show the character commenting on how the problem was solved.
- Include a **reflection of what happened** - this shows the character is thinking about the situation and outcome.

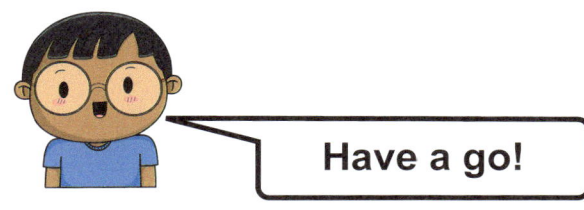

Have a go!

Look at the problems below. How could they be solved?
The first one has been done for you.

Problem	Solution
The character lost his wallet.	He searches everywhere and finds it in the car.
The character gets lost in the mountains.	
The character sees a shark whilst swimming in the sea.	
The character falls into a river whilst out walking her dog.	
The character is scared of going on a plane.	
The character went skiing but there was an avalanche.	
A dragon is guarding the castle that the character wants to visit.	
The character has a fight with their best friend.	
The character is chased by a scary creature.	
The character is home alone at night and hears a scary noise.	

Wrap it up!

Write the solution section for one of the problems on the previous page. Think about the features that you need to include - use the checklist to help you.

- A range of sentence starters
- Alliteration
- Synonyms of verbs
- Similes
- Body language
- Reflection of what happened
- Dialogue

Openings

Dialogue

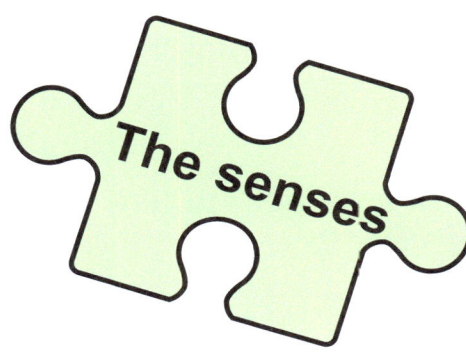

Solutions

Problems

Sentence starters

How to use this section

Talk together!

In this section you will be using all of the skills you have learned to write your own short stories.

There are four story titles:
- The race.
- Journey into space.
- The wizard.
- The camping trip.

You can complete them in any order that you want.

With each of the story titles there is an image to help generate ideas about the **character** and **setting**. There are also some questions to help you think about the **plot**.

Once you have completed this task you will be able to use all of the ideas to fill in the **planning grid**. Remember to **include** the **literary devices** and **sentence starters** on your plan.

When you have finalised the plan you will have everything needed to begin writing your story. There is a **checklist** at the top of the page to remind you of the **key elements** that need to be included.

On completion of your story, **read** and **check** that you have included everything on the checklist. You also need to check for **spelling** and **punctuation**.

On page 94 there is a list of 24 other story titles for you to 'Have a go!' at.

You can photocopy the planning grid and writing checklist on pages 102/103 to help you with your story writing.

Now you are ready to develop your own story titles!

Go ahead and have some fun writing your own short stories!

The race

Have a go!

Before you begin writing your story look at the image above. Answer the questions below. They will help you think about your plot.

- Who is the character?
- What are they racing?
- Where is the race happening?

- How does the character feel? (Why?)

- What problem does the character experience?

- How do they solve the problem?

- Who wins the race?

Use this grid to plan your story. First think about the plot and then add in all of the literary devices in the language boxes.

The opening	The problem	The solution
Plot		
Language		

Use the planning grid to write your story.
Use the checklist list to check that you have included everything.

Expanded noun phrase	Simile	Onomatopoeia	Alliteration
Personification	Body language	The senses	Sentence starters
Paragraphs	Punctuation	Dialogue	Suspense/Tension

Journey into space

Have a go!

Before you begin writing your story look at the image above. Answer the questions below. They will help you think about your plot.

- Who is in the spacecraft?
  _____
  _____

- Where are they going?
  _____
  _____

- Will they get there safely?
  _____
  _____

- What might they encounter on the way? (Problem)
  _____
  _____

- How do they solve the problem?
  _____
  _____

- How does the character feel about being in space?
  _____
  _____

Use this grid to plan your story. First think about the plot and then add in all of the literary devices in the language boxes.

The opening	The problem	The solution
Plot		
Language		

Use the planning grid to write your story.
Use the checklist to check that you have included everything.

Expanded noun phrase	Simile	Onomatopoeia	Alliteration
Personification	Body language	The senses	Sentence starters
Paragraphs	Punctuation	Dialogue	Suspense/Tension

_____
_____
_____
_____
_____
_____
_____
_____
_____
_____
_____
_____
_____
_____
_____
_____
_____
_____
_____
_____

The wizard

Have a go!

Before you begin writing your story look at the image above. Answer the questions below. They will help you think about your plot.

- Who is the character?
  _____
  _____

- Why is he there?
  _____
  _____

- What is he doing?
  _____
  _____

- Where is he going?
  _____
  _____

- What problem does he have on the way?
  _____
  _____

- How does he solve the problem?
  _____
  _____

Use this grid to plan your story. First think about the plot and then add in all of the literary devices in the language boxes.

The opening	The problem	The solution
Plot		
Language		

Use the planning grid to write your story.
Use the checklist to check that you have included everything.

Expanded noun phrase	Simile	Onomatopoeia	Alliteration
Personification	Body language	The senses	Sentence starters
Paragraphs	Punctuation	Dialogue	Suspense/Tension

The camping trip

Have a go!

Before you begin writing your story look at the image above. Answer the questions below. They will help you think about your plot.

- Who are the characters?
  _____
  _____

- Where are they?
  _____
  _____

- Why are they there?
  _____
  _____

- What are they doing?
  _____
  _____

- What problem do they encounter during the trip?
  _____
  _____

- How do they solve the problem?
  _____
  _____

Use this grid to plan your story. First think about the plot and then add in all of the literary devices in the language boxes.

The opening	The problem	The solution
Plot		
Language		

Use the planning grid to write your story.
Use the checklist to check that you have included everything.

Expanded noun phrase	Simile	Onomatopoeia	Alliteration
Personification	Body language	The senses	Sentence starters
Paragraphs	Punctuation	Dialogue	Suspense/Tension

Other story titles you can use

Wrap it up!

Here are some titles that you could use for your stories. Ask yourself questions about the characters and setting before you begin writing. Plan them in the same way that you have been doing.

• The lost key	• The jungle adventure
• The mysterious journey	• The lost island
• The talent show	• Home alone
• The flying car	• The shipwreck
• The stargazer	• The missing treasure
• The mysterious house	• The picnic
• Lost in the woods	• The secret tunnel
• The stormy night	• The strange visitors
• Behind the door	• On the beach
• The magic castle	• The game
• The ice palace	• The evil queen
• Ben's first day at school	• The magic phone

You might decide that you want to use an image to inspire your story.

Colour alternatives

red
- cherry
- rose
- crimson
- scarlet
- blood
- ruby
- berry

blue
- cyan
- ultramarine
- cobalt
- sapphire
- navy
- azure
- royal

yellow
- canary
- lemon
- golden
- mustard
- butterscotch
- dandelion
- honey

pink
- fuchsia
- magenta
- blossom
- salmon
- coral
- flamingo
- rose

Purple
- amethyst
- lavender
- plum
- blackcurrant
- violet
- lilac
- periwinkle

brown
- mocha
- peanut
- cinnamon
- chocolate
- tawny
- walnut
- caramel

green
- emerald
- olive
- moss
- avocado
- fern
- sage
- pistachio

black/grey
- soot
- ebony
- obsidian
- charcoal
- ash
- pewter
- graphite

orange
- carrot
- amber
- ginger
- tangerine
- marmalade
- marigold
- apricot

Adjective synonyms

Small
little	delicate
tiny	undersized
minute	weeny
minuscule	poky
mini	pocket-sized
miniature	puny
bijou	dinky
microscopic	teeny
compact	cramped

Big
large	jumbo
massive	gargantuan
gigantic	oversized
humongous	vast
mammoth	epic
huge	mega
ample	mighty
immense	whopping
monumental	colossal
substantial	tremendous

Good
excellent	splendid
marvellous	acceptable
super	stupendous
superb	amazing
exceptional	satisfying
magnificent	fantastic

Bad
awful	wretched
vile	ominous
horrific	dire
dreadful	offensive
rotten	unpleasant
loathsome	beastly

Cold
chilly	frosty
freezing	shivering
icy	crisp
bitter	wintry
sub-zero	glacial
biting	nippy

Hot
warm	sweltering
boiling	humid
roasting	baking
blistering	sizzling
tropical	balmy
summery	muggy

Old
ancient	frayed
elderly	senior
historic	worn
mature	weathered
tattered	antique

New
modern	unique
contemporary	fresh
pristine	untouched
unused	untried
current	brand new
recent	cutting edge

Body language

angry / annoyed
* red face
* eyes raging
* muttering under breath
* stomping
* folded arms
* shouting
* heart thumping
* lips pursed
* clenched jaw
* clenched fists
* sighing

embarrassed
* cheeks burning
* looking down
* avoid looking at anyone
* sweating
* touching head
* covering eyes
* arms folded across the chest
* fidgeting

sad / upset
* crying / tears
* shoulders slumped
* red eyes
* dragging feet
* heart pounding
* rubbing eyes
* blowing nose
* head hanging
* looking at the ground

excited
* wide eyes
* eyes bulging
* heart pounding
* waving arms
* big smile

shy
* looking down
* arms crossed
* standing alone
* quiet
* avoiding looking at anyone
* butterflies in tummy

tired
* yawning
* arms stretching
* droopy eyes
* blurry sight
* heavy body
* slow steps
* dragging feet

scared
* wobbly legs
* shaking
* goosebumps
* cover eyes
* eyes closed
* heart pounding
* breathing fast
* face turns white

happy
* sparkling eyes
* rosy cheeks
* laughing
* big smile
* face beaming
* waving arms
* talking to others
* skipping

nervous
* butterflies in tummy
* biting nails
* fingers in mouth
* fiddling with hair
* legs shaking
* sweating
* fidgeting

Words linked to the senses

Sight
- angular
- bent
- crooked
- clean
- gleaming
- glowing
- bright
- dull
- elegant
- flickering
- dazzling
- fluffy
- ghastly
- grotesque
- filthy
- dirty
- spotty
- stripey
- crinkled
- colourful
- fancy
- distinct
- crowded
- deserted

Hearing
- echoing
- raspy
- cacophony
- muffled
- soft
- silent
- soundless
- quiet
- hushed
- noisy
- loud
- raucous
- bellowing
- hoarse
- deafening
- scratching
- scuffling
- shuffling
- ticking
- melodic
- tuneful
- blood-curdling
- ear-splitting
- tormented

Touch
- abrasive
- bumpy
- lumpy
- cold
- prickly
- jagged
- knobbly
- bushy
- craggy
- supple
- cushioned
- waxy
- smooth
- velvety
- silky
- spongy
- sodden
- soaking
- moist
- damp
- itchy
- slippery
- sticky
- frozen

Taste
- acidic
- bitter
- ginger
- delicious
- gooey
- juicy
- sticky
- savoury
- salty
- sour
- sweet
- tangy
- tart
- vinegary
- bland
- seasoned
- flavoursome
- pungent
- peppery
- creamy

Smell
- aromatic
- delicious
- earthy
- musty
- pungent
- rancid
- putrid
- reeking
- odorous
- stinky
- flowery
- choking
- nauseating
- woody
- rotten
- sweet
- stale
- fresh
- vile
- bitter

Verb synonyms

Look	**Run**	**Walk**	**Laugh**
peer	sprint	stroll	chuckle
see	bolt	amble	giggle
gaze	zoom	trek	snigger
gape	jog	plod	titter
glance	pelt	march	chortle
glimpse	hurry	stride	howl
peek	scurry	troop	cackle
survey	charge	saunter	jeer
study	gallop	wander	hoot
spot	hurtle	tread	roar
observe	scamper	traipse	crack up
inspect	race	roam	fall about
examine	dart	hike	
gawp	trot	tramp	

Get	**Eat**	**Go**	**Find**
acquire	consume	move	discover
gain	devour	advance	notice
receive	chew	proceed	observe
obtain	demolish	progress	detect
gather	tuck into	travel	realise
earn	chomp	journey	note
purchase	guzzle	continue	learn
collect	swallow	leave	locate
accept	munch	visit	spot
pick up	ingest	depart	unearth
	dine		obtain
	feast		track down

Emotion words

Happy	Fear	Caring
Amused Buoyant Calm Cheerful Contented Delighted Ecstatic Elated Enthusiastic Exhilarated Grateful Jovial Jubilant Lively Merry Overjoyed Pleased Satisfied Thrilled	Distressed Frightened Horrified Paralyzed Petrified Shocked Terrified Afraid Alarmed Apprehensive Fearful Nervous Scared Anxious Cautious Worried	Accepted Affectionate Appreciated Attentive Blessed Cherished Compassionate Considerate Devoted Friendly Reassured Sympathetic Thoughtful Tolerant Trusting

Sadness	Confused	Angry
Ashamed Dejected Disappointed Discouraged Distressed Fed up Gloomy Hopeless Miserable Regretful Somber Sorrowful Tearful Unhappy Upset	Baffled Bewildered Distracted Disturbed Doubtful Embarrassed Flustered Frustrated Hesitant Misunderstood Puzzled Shy Startled Stumped Stunned Uncertain	Agitated Annoyed Bitter Cranky Disgusted Dismayed Exasperated Fed up Fuming Furious Grouchy Infuriated Livid Raging Seething

Adverbs of manner

adventurously	elegantly	jubilantly	rapidly
beautifully	enthusiastically	loyally	reassuringly
bravely	excitedly	neatly	successfully
carefully	fondly	obediently	sympathetically
cautiously	generously	optimistically	tremendously
cheerfully	gleefully	patiently	truthfully
daintily	honestly	politely	victoriously
diligently	jovially	positively	wisely
eagerly	joyfully	promptly	wonderfully

accidentally	hard	mysteriously	tastefully
briskly	hurriedly	physically	thoughtfully
busily	idealistically	punctually	tightly
closely	interestingly	randomly	unexpectedly
curiously	inquisitively	rashly	urgently
daringly	keenly	seriously	vaguely
deliberately	knowingly	sleepily	vastly
enormously	loudly	solemnly	wildly
extremely	mechanically	speedily	youthfully

anxiously	ferociously	madly	selfishly
awkwardly	fiercely	miserably	sternly
bashfully	foolishly	nervously	stupidly
bleakly	frantically	obnoxiously	suspiciously
carelessly	hastily	offensively	terribly
cruelly	hopelessly	recklessly	unfortunately
deceivingly	inadequately	reluctantly	unimpressively
defiantly	jealously	rudely	violently
doubtfully	lazily	sadly	worriedly

Synonyms for said

Said loudly
shouted, screamed, yelled, howled, cried, shrieked, roared, squealed, bellowed, hollered

Said quietly
whispered, murmured, muttered, mumbled, squeaked, whimpered, wheezed

Said funnily
cackled, giggled, sniggered, chortled, chuckled

Said angrily
growled, snapped, ranted, reprimanded, roared, nagged, pestered, berated, scolded, chastised

Conversations
asked, queried, questioned, declared, replied, insisted, answered, snapped, enquired, exclaimed, responded, chatted, argued, babbled

Said sadly
cried, snivelled, whimpered, wheezed, wept, bawled, whined, stammered, wailed, sobbed, groaned, blubbered

Making suggestions
suggested, remarked, exclaimed, recommended, encouraged, implied

Giving more details
explained, elaborated, continued, added, commented

	The opening	The problem	The solution
Plot			
Language			

Use the planning grid to write your story.
Use the checklist to check that you have included everything.

Expanded noun phrase	Simile	Onomatopoeia	Alliteration
Personification	Body language	The senses	Sentence starters
Paragraphs	Punctuation	Dialogue	Suspense/Tension

Answers section

Answers

Pg9

Correct expanded noun phrases:

1. The girl had **some sparkly, pink shoes** that she wore to the disco.
2. **The stripey, blue fish** swim quickly through the ocean.
3. The man drove **his rusty, old van** slowly down the road.
4. My grandmother lives in **a pretty, little cottage**.
5. The boy brought **a new, fluffy jacket**.
6. **The one-eyed, green alien** landed his silver spaceship.
7. **The bright green, wooden door** slowly creaked open.
8. On Tuesday, **the young, mischievous boy** went to the park.
9. For dinner, I had **some delicious, creamy soup**.

Select suitable adjectives to describe the noun.

Pg10

Select suitable expanded noun phrases linked to the picture. These could be about the **rocks, mountains, snow, water or sky**.

Pg13

The correct similes are underlined and the nouns are in bold:

1. The roaring **fire** is as bright as the **sun**.
2. The **freezer** was as cold as an **ice cube**.
3. The **water** is cold like **ice**.
4. The **doctor** was as busy as a **bee**.
5. My **mum** is busy like a **beaver**.
6. The **stars** are as twinkly as **diamonds**.
7. The **lights** were bright like **stars**.
8. The **car** was speeding down the road as fast as a **rocket**.

Make sure the similes include suitable comparisons.

Pg14

Select suitable similes linked to the picture. These could be about the **leaves, path, or trees**.

Pg16

For the onomatopoeia you could include some of the words below:

Fall over and hurt your knee - **Ouch! Crash! Groan.**
A cow on a farm - **Moo.**
A police car - **Woo woo! Wee woo! Nee naw!**
A door being slammed - **Bang! Thud! Crash! Slam!**
Children playing a musical instrument - **Ding! Bang! Twang! Clink! Clank! Chime!**
Taking a drink of juice - **Slurp! gurgle! gulp!**
A doorbell - **Ding dong! Ring! Buzz!**

For the onomatopoeia the answers are:

1. I hit the ground with a **thud.**
2. The window broke with a loud **smash.**
3. The thunder **rumbled** in the sky.
4. The water **gurgles** down the drainpipe.
5. The branches **snap** in the wind.
6. The waves **crashed** against the side of the ship.
7. The egg was **sizzling** in the pan.
8. There was a loud **bang** and everything went dark.

Pg17

Ammar has not underlined the onomatopoeia in the sentence.
Woof! Is the correct onomatopoeia because it is a sound an animal would make.

Kayleigh has underlined **squeak** - this is the correct answer because it is a sound an animal would make.

Emily has not included an onomatopoeia in her writing. Quietly is an adverb not an onomatopoeia.

Pg19

Make sure your answers all include the same sound at the beginning of the word.
You could include:
The weird, wicked wizard.
The mighty, magnificent mountains.
The beautiful buzzing bees.

Pg20

Select suitable alliteration linked to the picture. These could be about the **trees, mountains, snow or sky.**

Pg22

Correct personified words are in **bold** and correct verbs are underlined
1. The **sun** sang in the sky.
2. My **alarm** clock yelled at me to get up.
3. The **clouds** danced across the sky.
4. The still **water** shivered in the wind.
5. The sky was full of dancing **stars**.
6. The **snow** whispered as it fell from the sky.
7. The car **engine** coughed in the cold morning.
8. The **kettle** whistled a joyful tune.
9. The **waves** gently tickled her toes as she stood on the shore.

For the second part of page 22 - When you are adding your own verbs use your knowledge accordingly. Here are some examples:

1. Shivered.
2. Stood.
3. Crying.
4. Screaming.
5. Laughed.
6. Danced.
7. Wrapped.

Pg23

The waves crashed against the boat - **Gloomy**.
The rays of sun danced through the leaves - **Happy**.
The lightening smashed the city with its bolts - **Gloomy**.
The trees whispered in the breeze - **Happy**.
The waves gently stroked the shore - **Happy**.
The car's headlights glared at me - **Gloomy**.
The leaves waved in the wind - **Happy**.
The sun peered through the trees - **Happy**.
The waves angrily slapped the side of the ship - **Gloomy**.
Lightening danced across the sky - **Happy**.
Hailstones thumped against the window - **Gloomy**.
My alarm clock screamed at me to wake up - **Gloomy**.
The snowflakes pirouette in the sky - **Happy**.
The sun screamed in the sky - **Gloomy**.
Trees swayed in the wind - **Happy**.
The car's headlights winked at me - **Happy**.
The leaves danced in the wind - **Happy**.
The waves tickled her toes - **Happy**.
The flowers were begging for water - **Gloomy**.
Waves ran across the sand - **Happy**.
My warm coat hugged me - **Happy**.

Pg24

Select suitable personification linked to the picture. These could be about the **trees, plants, rocks and water.**

Pg26

Body language answers:

Excited: wide eyes, heart pounding, jumping up and down, waving arms.
Tired: yawning, dragging feet, droopy eyes, quiet, arms stretching.
Sad / upset: shoulders slumped, crying, stomping, red eyes, blowing nose, shouting.
Nervous: Legs shaking, heart pounding, fiddling with hair, looking down, biting nails, butterflies in tummy.
Angry / annoyed: Arms crossed, stomping, red face, shouting, clenched fists, red eyes.
Shy: Rosy cheeks, arms crossed, standing alone, looking down, cover eyes, biting nails, quiet.
Scared: wide eyes, goose bumps, legs shaking, heart pounding, cover eyes, biting nails, face turns white.
Happy: Laughing, face beaming, sparkling eyes, waving arms, rosy cheeks.

Pg27

Use suitable body language for the emotions shown in the pictures.
Picture 1: She could be **scared** or **anxious**.
Picture 2: She could be **happy** or **excited**.

Pg29

The rough bark - **touch**.
The luminous paint - **sight**.
The pleasant aroma - **smell**.
The spotty jumper - **sight**.
The sodden blanket - **touch**.
The clear glass - **sight**.
The bland potatoes - **taste**.
The putrid smoke - **smell**.
The smooth steel - **touch**.
The snarling dogs - **hearing**.
The abrasive sandpaper - **touch**.
The pungent garlic - **smell**.
The savoury biscuit - **taste**.
The creaking door - **hearing**.
The fragrant flowers - **smell**.
The tart lemons - **taste**.
The clattering plates - **hearing**.
The spicy curry - **taste**.
The wailing baby - **hearing**.
The prickly bush - **touch**.
The greasy sausages - **taste**.
The aromatic oil - **smell**.
The rustling leaves - **hearing**.
The flashing lights - **sight**.
The stench of rotten cabbage - **smell**.
The glowing eyes - **sight**.
The appetising cakes - **taste**.
The chirping birds - **hearing**.
The dazzling lights - **sight**.
The gritty sand - **touch**.
The jagged rocks - **touch**.

Pg30

Select suitable sensory description linked to the picture. It could be about the **water, mountains, trees or sky.**

Pg33

I went to the park <u>on Tuesday afternoon</u> - **Phrase**
<u>The dog sat</u> on a mat in the garden - **Clause**.
The children run <u>around the park</u> - **Phrase.**
<u>We are visiting the castle</u> near the park - **Clause**.

The cheerful lady works <u>in the office</u> - **Phrase**.
The children watch television <u>after they had eaten their dinner</u> - **Clause**.
<u>The grumpy, old man</u> slipped down the stairs - **Phrase**.
<u>The fox was hiding</u> in the thick, prickly hedge - **Clause**.
<u>On the brightly lit stage,</u> the boy began to play the guitar - **Phrase**.
Bursting into tears, <u>the boy ran</u> towards his home - **Clause**.
I gave my mum <u>a beautiful, antique ring</u> - **Phrase**.

Pg34

Adding a phrase to the main clause, these could be:
2. James watched the television **in the evening**.
3. Fatima ate her dinner **in the kitchen**.
4. The boy hid **behind the bike shed.**
5. **The cheeky young boy** wore a jumper.

Underlined prepositional phrases are:
1. We are going to the zoo <u>on Thursday.</u>
2. The boy hid <u>under the bed</u> when playing hide and seek.
3. I peered <u>though the window</u> to see the birds.
4. Sam put the heavy box <u>on the table</u>.
5. <u>At the weekend</u> Harry watched a film.
6. The lazy dog slept <u>in its bed</u>.

Pg36

Paul was tired so he went to bed - **Compound**.
Tomorrow, I am going on holiday - **Simple**.
After he has completed his homework, he will watch the television - **Complex**.
I wanted to swim in the sea but the water was too cold - **Compound**.
The boy wore a dirty jumper - **Simple**.
Harry turned off his light and went to sleep - **Compound**.
Before the film began, the children ate their popcorn - **Complex**.
Mick was playing on the computer - **Simple**.
The old man slipped over because it was icy outside - **Complex**.
Before we went to the shops, we made a list of what to buy - **Complex**.
I lost the key to the front door - **Simple**.
I lost the key to the front door so I couldn't get in - **Compound**.

Pg37

Use your knowledge of sentence structures to write about the picture.

Pg39

The where starters are underlined:
1. <u>On top of the hill,</u> there stood three exhausted figures.
2. <u>Beneath the water,</u> the fish swum happily.
3. <u>Behind the tree,</u> a little boy crouched silently.
4. <u>Under the bed,</u> the boy frantically searched for his torch.
5. <u>Beyond the town,</u> there stood an ancient castle.
6. <u>Near the supermarket,</u> an old lady sat on a bench.

The new sentences should be:
2. <u>From behind the building,</u> a cloaked figure appeared.
3. <u>Outside the gates,</u> the group of children waited.
4. <u>On the beach,</u> Mary sat happily building a sandcastle.
5. <u>From behind the door,</u> a loud scream echoed.
6. <u>On the other side of the wall,</u> the dog was frantically barking.

Pg40

There are several answers you could include, below are some examples:
1. <u>In the back garden,</u> the boys were playing football.
2. <u>Inside their nest,</u> the birds sang sweetly.
3. <u>Beside the garden fence,</u> Sam ate a strawberry lolly.

4. **Down by the seafront,** Jack was building sandcastles.
5. **Over by the lake,** I could see the mountain peaks.
6. **In the garden,** the children were making a plan.
7. **Next to the goalpost,** the footballer aimed for the goal.

There are several answers you could include, below are some examples:
1. In the distance, **there was a huge, grey elephant**.
2. Down by the river, **the children were catching fish**.
3. In the water, **the dolphins splashed around merrily**.
4. Somewhere close by, **the ghostly figure slowly crept**.

Pg42

The adverbials of time have been underlined below:
1. **In the middle of the night,** a strange sound could be heard outside.
2. **All of a sudden,** the door swung open.
3. **Last year,** Jack went on holiday to Spain.
4. **In the autumn,** the leaves fall off the trees.
5. **As soon as possible,** he leapt from the speeding car.
6. **In the blink of an eye,** it finished.

The new sentences should be:
2. **On Saturday,** the boys enjoyed playing football in the park.
3. **In the summer holidays,** the children went to the beach.
4. **In the middle of the night,** there was a loud bang.
5. **Early in the morning,** the children crept out of their beds.
6. **Late in the afternoon,** Mary went for a walk in the park.

Pg43

Below are some examples of suitable adverbials of time you could use:
1. **In the afternoon,** the girls watched a film.
2. **Later that evening,** the dog howled loudly.
3. **Afterwards,** Fred was eating his tea.
4. **At the stroke of midnight,** a dark figure appeared.
5. **After breakfast,** I walked to the shops.
6. **In July,** I celebrated my birthday.
7. **In the winter,** it was dark.

Below are some examples of main clauses that you could use:
1. At midnight, **we had a secret party**.
2. On Thursday morning, **it was very hot**.
3. In the middle of winter, **all the hedgehogs hibernate**.
4. Later in the afternoon, **we are allowed to play with our toys**.

Pg45

Below are some examples of an emotion adjective that you could use:
1. **Jubilant,** Hannah ran as fast as she could.
2. **Excited,** Nivi ripped open his present.
3. **Angry,** Eloise shouted at her younger sister.
4. **Exhilarated,** Ryan kicked the ball to the back of the goal.
5. **Terrified,** Anya hid under her bed.
6. **Bemused,** Nathan stared at the figure in front of him.

Below are some examples of sentences that could come after the emotion word:
1. Confused, **Mable wondered where she had lost her keys**.

2. Horrified, **the man ran away from the dark figure**.
3. Furious, **Paul threw his broken toy on the ground**.
4. Delighted, **the girls giggled at the cake**.
5. Infuriated, **she clenched her fists in anger**.
6. Nervous, **he took a step back from the barking dog**.
7. Startled, **James awoke with a fright**.
8. Jubilant, **the team cheered loudly when they won**.

Pg46

No, Emily has not underlined the emotion word. Ripped is a verb. **Delighted** is the correct emotion word.

No, Kaylee has not used an emotion word starter, she has used a **when** (adverb of time) sentence starter.

No, Sam has used an emotion word, but not the correct one for the sentence. If someone is skipping across the playground it would suggest they are **happy** not terrified.

Pg48

The 'ing' and 'who' words have been underlined below, also the comma has been included:
1. **Gazing** out of the window, **Harry** saw two cars collide.
2. **Drawing** his sword, the **knight** went into battle.
3. **Noticing** the commotion, the **children** ran to see what was going on outside.
4. **Feeling** tired, **Dave** fell asleep at the cinema.
5. **Sprinting** quickly, **Anna** grabbed the prize.
6. **Wailing** in pain, **Steven** limped towards the door.
7. **Leaping** into the water, **Jack** made a huge splash.
8. **Moving** quickly, **they** could sense the danger ahead.
9. **Staring** into space, **she** had lost track of time.
10. **Listening** carefully to the instructions, **James** completed the task.

Below are some examples of suitable **main clauses with a comma**. **Who** is also included:
1. Screaming in pain, **Tamwar** held his broken arm.
2. Breathing heavily, **the runners** sprinted by.
3. Feeling excited, **the twins** ran to find their presents.
4. Moving quickly, **the car** drove past the people.
5. Lurking in the darkness, **monsters** peered around the corner.
6. Looking behind her, **Samantha** saw her friends arriving.
7. Treading carefully, **Gemma** tiptoed over the wet grass.
8. Scrambling through the bushes, **the children** hoped to find treasure.

Pg49

Emily has not used an 'ing' starter, she has used a **when** starter (an adverb of time).

You could have used **breathing heavily**, or **running**, or any other suitable 'ing' word.

Sam has not used a suitable 'ing' word as screaming in pain would suggest Zoe was not happy.

Pg51

Correct adverbs of manner and commas are:
2. **Victoriously and enthusiastically,** Ella sprinted over the finish line.
3. **Aggressively waving his sword,** the knight charged.
4. **Nervously walking towards the door,** Jim looked to see if anyone was around.
5. **Unexpectedly,** a huge dog hurtled towards the children.
6. **Recklessly and defiantly,** he sped through the red light.

7. **Gleefully and joyfully,** Molly skipped along the road.
8. **Ridiculously lost and not knowing where to turn,** Adam finally got out the map.

Suitable main clauses and a comma could be:
1. Calmly working out what to do next, **he made his decision and left the building.**
2. Bravely and reassuringly, **the soldier helped the children escape.**
3. Energetically, **James worked out in the gym.**
4. Frustratedly looking at his watch, **Billy hoped his tea would be ready.**
5. Suspiciously, **the boys quickly left the sweet shop.**

Pg52

Kaylee has **not** used an adverb of manner, she has used a **when** starter (an adverb of time).

A suitable adverb of manner for Emilys sentence could be: **Carefully,** or **silently,**

Ammar has **not** used a suitable adverb of manner. You would not fiercely smile at someone. The correct sentence could say: **Happily,** the lady smiled at James.

Pg54

He loved to eat ice cream does not belong in the paragraph because it is a different topic.

The sentences are written in the incorrect order, it should be:
Sally lazily got out of bed. She quickly rushed to the bathroom and brushed her teeth. She hurried downstairs and grabbed her bag before heading out the door.

Pg55

The new paragraph needs to start with the sentence: **When they arrived at the shop, they dashed towards the fridge.**

Make your own decisions about literary devices that have been added.

Pg57

Make your own decision about the writing, your answers need to include the **senses.**

Pg58

Make your own decision about the writing, your answers need to include the **senses** and a **range of literary devices.**

Pg60

Use your own ideas to answer the questions about the character.
In the second part make sure that you are focused on the character's **actions.**

Pg61

Make sure that you are focused on the character's **actions, personality** and that you have given them a **name.**

Pg63

The fire brigade put the fire out - **solution**. The volcano erupted - **problem**. A family go out for a drive - **opening**. The boy fell into the lake - **problem**. The children got lost on the beach and could not find their parents - **problem**. The car speeds towards the cliff edge - **problem**. The children went to the seaside - **opening**. The driver manages to press the brakes - **solution**. The family left and went to a safe place - **solution**. Max was in the bedroom playing with matches - **opening**. She climbs on the rocks to get to somewhere safe - **solution**. Their parents found them and they went for an ice cream - **solution**. There was a cheeky boy called Tom playing by a lake - **opening**. Lisa was in a boat on the sea - **opening**. The house caught fire - **problem**. A passer-by sees a boy in the lake and pulls him out - **solution**. A family went on holiday to Italy to visit a volcano - **opening**. The boat crashes in to the rocks - **problem**.

Below are the openings, problems and solutions that go together:

1. A family go out for a drive. The car speeds towards the cliff edge. The driver manages to press the brakes.
2. The children went to the seaside. The children got lost on the beach and could not find their parents. Their parents found them and they went for an ice cream.
3. Max was in the bedroom playing with matches. The house caught fire. The fire brigade put the fire out.
4. There was a cheeky boy called Tom playing by a lake. The boy fell into the lake. A passer-by sees a boy in the lake and pulls him out.
5. Lisa was in a boat on the sea. The boat crashes in to the rocks. She climbs on the rocks to get to somewhere safe.
6. A family went on holiday to Italy to visit a volcano. The volcano erupted. The family left and went to a safe place.

Pg65

Select suitable **literary devices** and **sentence starters** for the story you have selected.

Pg67

If you are creating a character opening, focus on the **actions** of the character and give **clues** about the **setting**.
If you are creating a description opener try to include the **senses** and introduce the **character** towards the end of the paragraph.

Pg68

Your opening should include **similes, alliteration, onomatopoeia, personification, the senses** and should also introduce the **character** and **setting**.

Pg70

These are some of the features that could be underlined:
Descriptions of surroundings - this has been completed for you.
Body language - began to tremble, palms were clammy, sweat ran down his face.
Ellipses - after the word looked.
Clues - dread filling his body, sweat ran down his face.
Senses - rancid smell of smoke, thick fumes, cracking flames, smash, the cold night air.
Include the weather - The cold night air.
Short sentences - He drew a breath. Max began to tremble. His palms were clammy.
Synonyms - fumes, edged, engulfing, screamed, raging, shooting.
Onomatopoeia - wheeze, crackling, smash, cracked.
Longer complex sentences - The rancid smell of smoke started to fill the air causing him to wheeze. As the crackling flames roared louder engulfing the room, Max began to tremble. The cold night air blew into the bedroom sending the red-hot flames shooting towards Max.
Rhetorical questions - What had he done? How would he escape? Would help arrive in time?
Similes - As hot as the sun.

Pg71

Your problem needs to include some **description of the surrounding, give clues**, have **shorter sentences, body language, the senses, longer sentences, synonyms, rhetorical questions, onomatopoeia, similes** and **ellipses**.

Pg73

Your solutions for the problems could be:

The character get lost in the mountains - **Search and rescue find him and take him to safety.**
The character sees a shark whilst swimming in the sea - **He frantically swims to shore.**
The character falls into a river whilst out walking her dog - **The dog pulls her out of the water.**
The character is scared of going on a plane - **Her friend goes with her and calms her fears.**
The character went skiing but there was an avalanche - **He decides to ski to the bottom of the mountain.**
A dragon is guarding the castle that the character wants to visit - **A brave knight fights the dragon and enters the castle.**
The character has a fight with their best friend - **They soon make up and are friends again.**
The character is chased by a scary creature - **They manage to loose the creature in the woods.**
The character is home alone at night and hears a scary noise - **they quickly hide under the bed until their parents get home.**

Pg74

Your solution needs to include a range of **sentence starters, alliteration, verb synonyms, similes, body language, reflection of what happened** and **dialogue**.

For the stories that start on **page 77**, use your own judgement and check they include the following:
Expanded noun phrases.
Similes.
Onomatopoeia.
Alliteration.
Personification.
Body language.
The senses.
A range of sentence starters.
Is written in paragraphs.
Includes punctuation.
Dialogue.
Includes suspense and tension.